GW00670946

Francis Frith's
Around Sutton

Photographic Memories

Francis Frith's
Around Sutton

Martin Andrew

THE FRANCIS FRITH COLLECTION

FRITH BOOK Co

First published in the United Kingdom in 2001 by
Frith Book Company Ltd

Paperback Edition 2001
ISBN 1-85937-337-2

Text and Design copyright © Frith Book Company Ltd
Photographs copyright © The Francis Frith Collection

The Frith photographs and the Frith logo are reproduced under licence from
Heritage Photographic Resources Ltd, the owners of the Frith archive and trademarks

All rights reserved. No photograph in this publication may be sold to a third party other than in
the original form of this publication, or framed for sale to a third party.
No parts of this publication may be reproduced, stored in a retrieval system, or
transmitted, in any form, or by any means, electronic, mechanical, photocopying, recording or
otherwise, without the prior permission of the publishers and copyright holder.

British Library Cataloguing in Publication Data

Francis Frith's Around Sutton
Martin Andrew

Frith Book Company Ltd
Frith's Barn, Teffont,
Salisbury, Wiltshire SP3 5QP
Tel: +44 (0) 1722 716 376
Email: info@francisfrith.co.uk
www.francisfrith.co.uk

Printed and bound in Great Britain

Front Cover: Sutton, High Street c1960 s233076

AS WITH ANY HISTORICAL DATABASE THE FRITH ARCHIVE IS CONSTANTLY BEING CORRECTED AND IMPROVED
AND THE PUBLISHERS WOULD WELCOME INFORMATION ON OMISSIONS OR INACCURACIES

Contents

Francis Frith: *Victorian Pioneer*

FRANCIS FRITH, Victorian founder of the world-famous photographic archive, was a complex and multi-talented man. A devout Quaker and a highly successful Victorian businessman, he was both philosophic by nature and pioneering in outlook.

By 1855 Francis Frith had already established a wholesale grocery business in Liverpool, and sold it for the astonishing sum of £200,000, which is the equivalent today of over £15,000,000. Now a multi-millionaire, he was able to indulge his passion for travel. As a child he had pored over travel books written by early explorers, and his fancy and imagination had been stirred by family holidays to the sublime mountain regions of Wales and Scotland. 'What a land of spirit-stirring and enriching scenes and places!' he had written. He was to return to these scenes of grandeur in later years to 'recapture the thousands of vivid and tender memories', but with a different purpose. Now in his thirties, and captivated by the new science of photography, Frith set out on a series of pioneering journeys to the Nile regions that occupied him from 1856 until 1860.

Intrigue and Adventure

He took with him on his travels a specially-designed wicker carriage that acted as both dark-room and sleeping chamber. These far-flung journeys were packed with intrigue and adventure. In his life story, written when he was sixty-three, Frith tells of being held captive by bandits, and of fighting 'an awful midnight battle to the very point of surrender with a deadly pack of hungry, wild dogs'. Sporting flowing Arab costume, Frith arrived at Akaba by camel seventy years before Lawrence, where he encountered 'desert princes and rival sheikhs, blazing with jewel-hilted swords'.

During these extraordinary adventures he was assiduously exploring the desert regions bordering the Nile and patiently recording the antiquities and peoples with his camera. He was the first photographer to venture beyond the sixth cataract. Africa was still the mysterious 'Dark Continent', and Stanley and Livingstone's historic meeting was a decade into the future. The conditions for picture taking confound belief. He laboured for hours in his wicker dark-room in the sweltering heat of the desert, while the volatile chemicals fizzed dangerously in their trays. Often he was forced to work in remote tombs and caves where conditions were cooler. Back in London he exhibited his photographs and was 'rapturously cheered' by members of the Royal Society. His reputation as a photographer was made overnight. An eminent modern historian has likened their impact on the population of the time to that on our own generation of the first photographs taken on the surface of the moon.

Venture of a Life-Time

Characteristically, Frith quickly spotted the opportunity to create a new business as a specialist publisher of photographs. He lived in an era of immense and sometimes violent change. For the poor in the early part of Victoria's reign work was a drudge and the hours long, and people had precious little free time to enjoy themselves. Most had no transport other than a cart or gig at their disposal, and had not travelled far beyond the boundaries of their own town or village. However,

by the 1870s, the railways had threaded their way across the country, and Bank Holidays and half-day Saturdays had been made obligatory by Act of Parliament. All of a sudden the ordinary working man and his family were able to enjoy days out and see a little more of the world.

With characteristic business acumen, Francis Frith foresaw that these new tourists would enjoy having souvenirs to commemorate their days out. In 1860 he married Mary Ann Rosling and set out with the intention of photographing every city, town and village in Britain. For the next thirty years he travelled the country by train and by pony and trap, producing fine photographs of seaside resorts and beauty spots that were keenly bought by millions of Victorians. These prints were painstakingly pasted into family albums and pored over during the dark nights of winter, rekindling precious memories of summer excursions.

The Rise of Frith & Co

Frith's studio was soon supplying retail shops all over the country. To meet the demand he gathered about him a small team of photographers, and published the work of independent artist-photographers of the calibre of Roger Fenton and Francis Bedford. In order to gain some understanding of the scale of Frith's business one only has to look at the catalogue issued by Frith & Co in 1886: it runs to some 670 pages, listing not only many thousands of views of the British Isles but also many photographs of most European countries, and China, Japan, the USA and Canada – note the sample page shown above from the hand-written *Frith & Co* ledgers detailing pictures taken. By 1890 Frith had created the greatest specialist photographic publishing company in the world,

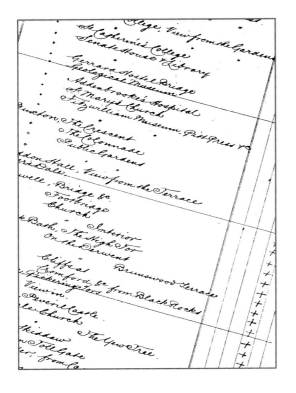

Frith's death, a new card measuring 5.5 x 3.5 inches became the standard format, but it was not until 1902 that the divided back came into being, with address and message on one face and a full-size illustration on the other. *Frith & Co* were in the vanguard of postcard development, and Frith's sons Eustace and Cyril continued their father's monumental task, expanding the number of views offered to the public and recording more and more places in Britain, as the coasts and countryside were opened up to mass travel.

Francis Frith died in 1898 at his villa in Cannes, his great project still growing. The archive he created continued in business for another seventy years. By 1970 it contained over a third of a million pictures of 7,000 cities, towns and villages. The massive photographic record Frith has left to us stands as a living monument to a special and very remarkable man.

with over 2,000 outlets – more than the combined number that Boots and W H Smith have today! The picture on the right shows the *Frith & Co* display board at Ingleton in the Yorkshire Dales. Beautifully constructed with mahogany frame and gilt inserts, it could display up to a dozen local scenes.

Postcard Bonanza

The ever-popular holiday postcard we know today took many years to develop. In 1870 the Post Office issued the first plain cards, with a pre-printed stamp on one face. In 1894 they allowed other publishers' cards to be sent through the mail with an attached adhesive halfpenny stamp. Demand grew rapidly, and in 1895 a new size of postcard was permitted called the court card, but there was little room for illustration. In 1899, a year after

Frith's Archive: *A Unique Legacy*

FRANCIS FRITH'S legacy to us today is of immense significance and value, for the magnificent archive of evocative photographs he created provides a unique record of change in 7,000 cities, towns and villages throughout Britain over a century and more. Frith and his fellow studio photographers revisited locations many times down the years to update their views, compiling for us an enthralling and colourful pageant of British life and character.

We tend to think of Frith's sepia views of Britain as nostalgic, for most of us use them to conjure up memories of places in our own lives with which we have family associations. It often makes us forget that to Francis Frith they were records of daily life as it was actually being lived in the cities, towns and villages of his day. The Victorian age was one of great and often bewildering change for ordinary people, and though the pictures evoke an impression of slower times, life was as busy and hectic as it is today.

We are fortunate that Frith was a photographer of the people, dedicated to recording the minutiae of everyday life. For it is this sheer wealth of visual data, the painstaking chronicle of changes in dress, transport, street layouts, buildings, housing, engineering and landscape that captivates us so much today. His remarkable images offer us a powerful link with the past and with the lives of our ancestors.

Today's Technology

Computers have now made it possible for Frith's many thousands of images to be accessed almost instantly. In the Frith archive today, each photograph is carefully 'digitised' then stored on a CD Rom. Frith archivists can locate a single photograph amongst thousands within seconds. Views can be catalogued and sorted under a variety of categories of place and content to the immediate benefit of researchers.

Inexpensive reference prints can be created for them at the touch of a mouse button, and a wide range of books and other printed materials assembled and published for a wider, more general readership - in the next twelve months over a hundred Frith local history titles will be published! The day-to-day workings of the archive are very different from how they were in Francis Frith's time: imagine the herculean task of sorting through eleven tons of glass negatives as Frith had to do to locate a particular sequence of pictures! Yet

See Frith at www.francisfrith.co.uk

the archive still prides itself on maintaining the same high standards of excellence laid down by Francis Frith, including the painstaking cataloguing and indexing of every view.

It is curious to reflect on how the internet now allows researchers in America and elsewhere greater instant access to the archive than Frith himself ever enjoyed. Many thousands of individual views can be called up on screen within seconds on one of the Frith internet sites, enabling people living continents away to revisit the streets of their ancestral home town, or view places in Britain where they have enjoyed holidays. Many overseas researchers welcome the chance to view special theme selections, such as transport, sports, costume and ancient monuments.

We are certain that Francis Frith would have heartily approved of these modern developments in imaging techniques, for he himself was always working at the very limits of Victorian photographic technology.

The Value of the Archive Today

Because of the benefits brought by the computer, Frith's images are increasingly studied by social historians, by researchers into genealogy and ancestory, by architects, town planners, and by teachers and schoolchildren involved in local history projects.

In addition, the archive offers every one of us an opportunity to examine the places where we and our families have lived and worked down the years. Highly successful in Frith's own era, the archive is now, a century and more on, entering a new phase of popularity.

The Past in Tune with the Future

Historians consider the Francis Frith Collection to be of prime national importance. It is the only archive of its kind remaining in private ownership and has been valued at a million pounds. However, this figure is now rapidly increasing as digital technology enables more and more people around the world to enjoy its benefits.

Francis Frith's archive is now housed in an historic timber barn in the beautiful village of Teffont in Wiltshire. Its founder would not recognize the archive office as it is today. In place of the many thousands of dusty boxes containing glass plate negatives and an all-pervading odour of photographic chemicals, there are now ranks of computer screens. He would be amazed to watch his images travelling round the world at unimaginable speeds through network and internet lines.

The archive's future is both bright and exciting. Francis Frith, with his unshakeable belief in making photographs available to the greatest number of people, would undoubtedly approve of what is being done today with his lifetime's work. His photographs, depicting our shared past, are now bringing pleasure and enlightenment to millions around the world a century and more after his death.

Sutton - *An Introduction*

I WAS DELIGHTED to be asked to select views and write about Sutton for the Frith photographic collection, as it covers a number of places I know very well indeed. In 1959, when I was twelve, my family moved from Ealing to Carshalton. I attended Sutton High School for Boys, and spent many a lunch hour walking around Sutton town centre and the surrounding area, often browsing in William Pile, the stationer and bookseller, which is on the corner of the High Street. We schoolboys walked in long crocodiles to the swimming baths in Throwley Road, or in the same crocodiles to school lunch in the Granada cinema's upstairs café, where lunch

cost half a crown. We played cricket and football at the sports fields in Cheam. On Saturdays my brother and I often went to Carshalton High Street, or walked to Wallington where there were some interesting shops, including a splendid stamp shop on Stafford Road.

My academic links with Sutton ceased in 1962 when the owner of the school, a Reverend Lawton, sold the 'prime development site' and closed the school, ending its 83 years of life. After my 'O' Levels, which I took at a Croydon school, (a town I have also covered in Frith's 'Living Memories' series) I went to Wallington Grammar School for

Boys. I was thus familiar with other parts of Wallington, including, I regret to admit, the Duke's Head on The Green, and Beddington. Our cross-country runs took us puffing as far as Mitcham Common. In those days, of course, Sutton was in the county of Surrey, but since 1965 it has been the centre of the London Borough of Sutton, which also incorporates Cheam, Carshalton (where my brother and his family still live), Wallington, Rose Hill, Beddington and part of Worcester Park, which are all covered in this book.

Although Sutton is shown as a bustling town in the views in this book, it was not always so. Until the mid-19th century it was merely one of a string of villages and hamlets along the spring line, where the chalk dips below a narrow belt of Thanet Sand before the start of the impervious London Clay on which London sits. Carshalton and its ponds are the clearest demonstration of this. Each parish was narrow and long from north to south. This arrangement gave each settlement an abundance of water, sheep and cow pasture, common grazing on the chalk Downs to the south, and arable land on the clay to the north. Sutton parish was, for example, about three miles long from north to south, and three quarters of a mile wide from east to west. There is a string of these strip parishes running from west to east, many of course now no longer separate parishes: Epsom, Ewell, Cuddington, Cheam, Sutton, Carshalton, Wallington, Beddington, Whaddon and Croydon.

The springs for the last five parishes collect to form the upper reaches of the River Wandle, one branch coming from the Ponds in Carshalton, the other from Croydon to Wallington, before turning north and meeting in Hackbridge to head for the River Thames.

These parishes emerged during the Middle Ages, but the story of Sutton begins long before that, with archaeological finds going back over ten thousand years. However, the first real substantial evidence of habitation came with the excavation of a Roman villa at Beddington. There have also been finds of burials, coins and artefacts in various parts of the area. On the ground, Stonecot Hill and London Road, the A24, runs along the course of Stane Street, which was the Roman road from London to Chichester. Moreover, Coldharbour Lane in Beddington is thought to have been a minor road in Roman times. These ancient roads formed part of the parish boundaries, which were established in the Anglo-Saxon period, the north boundary of Sutton following Stane Street, and the east boundary of Beddington parish following Coldharbour Lane.

However, it is with the arrival of the Anglo-Saxons, after the Romans left in the early 5th century AD, that our story really begins. The place names first appear in a charter of Chertsey Abbey, which appears to be a 13th-century copy and enlargement of one which is dated 727 AD, but was probably first drawn up fifty years before. This re-

copying and adapting was a common medieval practice during land disputes, and does not invalidate the earlier version, for parchment and paper decays and originals can get lost or destroyed. In any case, this charter gives us the first mention of several places covered in this book: Suthtone, Bedintone, Cegeham (Cheam) and Aeweltone (Carshalton). The charter lists lands given by one Frithwald to Chertsey Abbey. He was a Sub-Regulus or 'under-king' of Surrey.

Surrey had never been an independent Anglo-Saxon kingdom. It had been settled by the Middle Saxons, whose spoor is left in the old county name of Middlesex. Their territory seems to have crossed the River Thames to include Surrey or Suthrie, the southern region or area. Apparently, Surrey was variously controlled by Mercia and Wessex before finally being absorbed into Wessex after 825 AD, when King Egbert finally defeated Beornwulf of Mercia.

Chertsey Abbey was one of the richest and most powerful in England during the middle Ages, but virtually disappeared after the Dissolution of the monasteries by Henry VIII. Its stone was re-used by the king's masons at Nonsuch and Hampton Court palaces after 1538. This great Benedictine abbey was founded in 666, re-founded after Danish destruction in about 950, and the abbey was rebuilt after 1110. Chertsey Abbey held the manor of Sutton until its dissolution in 1537, when it was taken over by Henry VIII, who granted it to the Carews of Beddington. After various changes of ownership, the lordship of the manor was bought by Thomas Alcock in 1845. He sold part of the land for redevelopment, but also helped fund the fine new church of All Saints, Benhilton (1863-66), and the total rebuilding of St Nicholas, the parish church, in 1862-64. In 1912 the lordship was stripped of manorial rights, and sold to the Lamplugh family. The current Lord of the Manor is president of the Sutton and Cheam Society.

Until the middle of the 18th century, Sutton was of no greater size than any of the other villages along the spring line, and was considerably smaller than Epsom. It was focussed around The Green and the parish church some 800 yards to the south, but of this phase little if anything survived. The first catalyst for growth was the turnpiking of the London to Brighton road, which went through Sutton from 1755, turnpiking until 1809, after which the route moved east to go through Croydon. Even so, in the 1840s, around twenty coaches a day changed horses at the Cock Hotel. An east-west turnpike road was laid out at the same time, which ran from Epsom to Croydon. It passed through Sutton on the Carshalton and Cheam Roads, thus producing a major crossroads where development grew. There were toll gates by the crossroads for both routes until 1863, when they were relocated: one to the Gander Green Lane junction on Cheam Road, the other further south on the Brighton Road. The tolls were abolished in 1882. The Cock Hotel was built

near the crossroads, and the first view in this book shows it in its 18th-century state, before it was replaced in the 1890s. It then disappeared in the redevelopment-crazed 1960s.

What really made Sutton, however, was the arrival of the railway in 1847. The census population figures tell the story: 1,304 in 1841, 13,977 in 1891 and 21,270 in 1911. Sutton's neighbour Cheam, by contrast, saw its population grow from 1,109 in 1841 to 2,146 in 1891 and, with something of a spurt, rise to 6,200 by 1911. Sutton, a junction station from 1865, underwent spectacular growth, due not only to its railway station, but also its location at an important crossroads. The town rapidly lost its weather-boarded cottages, which were replaced by Victorian terraces of shops with first-storey flats. Many of these survived, together with other prosperous commercial buildings, such as the fine bank at the south-west corner of High Street and Cheam Road. The suburbs grew rapidly with the provision of essential services. The key to this development was the provision of piped water and mains drainage by the Sutton Water Company, which was founded in 1864, and the Sutton Gas Company in 1857.

There were several inns for the coaching trade. There was The Cock, which pre-dated the turnpiking of the London to Brighton road in the 1750s, but was rebuilt in the 1890s. The Greyhound, another old inn further down the High Street, was rebuilt in 1893. With the expansion of the village into a town, post-railway, the spiritual needs of the inhabitants were also considered and provided for. A number of churches were built, or in the case of the parish church of St Nicholas, rebuilt. Baptists, Roman Catholics, Congregationalists and Methodists were provided for, and more Anglican churches were built to serve the new suburbs. These were: All Saints for Benhilton in the 1860s, Christchurch for south Sutton in the 1880s and St Barnabas for east Sutton, also in the 1880s. Each suburb had a distinctive character, and the photographs in this book reflect these differences, with the tree-lined and spacious development of Benhilton being the most superior. East Sutton, however, had more of an artisan flavour. It is unfortunate that large numbers of these houses have gone, for from the 1950s onwards Sutton's commuter-land developers saw flats as the future. Large houses in spacious grounds were replaced by blocks of mostly three-storey flats. In some roads very few older houses survived, and in the case of Christchurch Park not one house survived the tide of flat building.

The early views in this book show Sutton from the 1890s, at the height of its Victorian prosperity, when the village had been transformed into a substantial commercial centre. This was surrounded by prosperous suburbs, which were still burgeoning. At this time the place was transformed from a parish into a Local Government District in 1882. In 1894 it became a fully-fledged

Urban District Council. As a consequence, in 1900 the town acquired Municipal Offices, which were at the junction of Throwley Road with the High Street. Public Baths, also in Throwley Road, followed in 1903. A modern post office was built in Grove Road in 1907, and a large police station in Carshalton Road in 1909. Schools, such as the County School, which was behind the Municipal Offices, were built in 1899. In 1906 trams arrived at the north end of town, later to be replaced by trolley buses.

The commercial centre prospered when Ernest Shinner opened his first shop in the High Street in 1899. By the 1930s, he had become so successful that he owned the whole of a terrace, and even bought out the Baptist church, which relocated to Cheam Road on the proceeds. William Pile's on the corner of Carshalton Road opened in 1883, and grew to be a popular landmark in the town. Cinemas were built: the Cheam Road Cinema in 1911, and the Surrey County Cinema in the High Street, later renamed the Gaumont. This was demolished in 1959. The Plaza in Carshalton Road was built in 1934; it later became the Granada, and was demolished in 1979. There were several private schools, some of which prospered, such as Sutton High School for Girls, founded in 1884. Some did not have so much success, such as Sutton High School for Boys, which was founded in 1879. It closed in 1962 and is now occupied by a Safeway's supermarket. Other schools that no longer exist are Woodside House School and Benhilton College,

both in Benhilton, and Eversfield School in Mulgrave Road.

The later views in this book capture the town just as the 1963 development plan started to bear its somewhat poisonous fruit. The key element was the pedestrianisation of much of the High Street. This was achieved by means of parallel roads to its east and west. These became Throwley Way and St Nicholas Way, which cut swathes through the hinterland and opened up many sites for redevelopment, ringing the town with new buildings. Some of it was in the form of tower office blocks. Much of the character of the town was swept way in the late 1960s and 1970s. This included the removal of the Municipal Offices, the swimming baths, the Congregational Church, the Granada cinema, Shinner's department store, Len's of Sutton, the Cock Hotel, the Greyhound and much else besides. In the suburbs, at the same time, blocks of bland flats were replacing the Victorian and Edwardian heritage. Thus the views in this book are a record of the town before this period of spectacular change.

The last two chapters comprise two short tours. The first one to the north and west is through an area radically changed from farmland by suburban expansion, filling in the gap between London and Sutton. Between the two World Wars, Worcester Park, Raynes Park, New Malden and the St Helier Estate at Rose Hill were built. Raynes Park follows the river Wandle and the spring line villages east of

Sutton, which expanded around historic cores, including Carshalton, Beddington and Wallington. However, the nucleus of this book is Sutton, a town that grew from a village, after the middle of the 19th century, to be a serious rival to Croydon, complete with commercial tower blocks.

I have many happy memories of Sutton, Carshalton and Wallington in the 1960s, and I am a frequent visitor to Carshalton, where my brother still lives. I enjoy looking around and seeing the changes, some regrettable and others good. Sutton is a vibrant, successful town, with two major shopping malls off its pedestrianised High Street. It is a civilised place to stroll around. I hope you enjoy this selection of views that capture the area very successfully, with views ranging from the 1890s into the mid 1960s.

The Town Centre

The Cock Hotel 1890 27423a
This superb view captures the character of old Sutton at its central crossroads. Here is the old Cock Hotel, complete with a Cycle Touring Club badge, and a hanging sign on a beam spanning the road. To the left is the old beer-house, known as the Cock Hotel Tap. Beyond, towards the station, there is still a large tree and a rural atmosphere. In the foreground was a tollgate, which was only removed in 1882, eight years before this view was taken.

The Cock Hotel 1898
41708
Eight years later, the Cock Hotel Tap building, (demolished in 1896), has been replaced by a spanking modern hotel, in an ornate sub-Norman Shaw style with oriel windows, plaster friezes, a deep cornice and a steep roof with high dormers. The corner is emphasised by a lead-roofed turret and cupola. The Cock Inn dated back at least to the early 17th century, and its 18th-century successor, the stuccoed Georgian building, was demolished soon after 1898.

High Street 1932 85075

By 1932 the Cock Hotel's sign had moved from the pavement to a traffic island, a location it still occupies today. On the opposite corner to Barclays Bank is the neo-Georgian Lloyds bank, and beyond it, stepping downhill, a terrace of shops built in 1870. The church tower seen on the left, with the parapet and pyramidal tiled roof, was the Baptist Church of 1886. This was demolished to make way for an extension to Shinner's department store in 1934.

The Bank 1900 45478

This bank is opposite the Cock Hotel, on the corner of Cheam Road. This grandiose building makes a splendid contrast to the ornate 1897 hotel building. It was built for the London and Provincial Bank in a French Renaissance style. It is now Barclays Bank, with the ground floor painted grey, and the upper storeys white. The 1890s Dutch/Flemish style building on the left is now O'Neill's pub, and was formerly the Railway Tavern. To the right, commerce has not yet reached Cheam Road.

Municipal Offices 1902 ▷
48864

Nearly opposite the Baptist Church, council offices were built in 1900 on the corner of Throwley Road. This befitted Sutton's status as an Urban District Council, which was granted in 1894. Its cupola can be seen in several views in this book, and its demolition in 1971 was a great loss. It was not as great a disaster for the character of the High Street as the truly dire concrete-framed Surrey House that replaced it and the school beyond. This dated from 1975 and is by R J Wood and Partners; it now looks horribly shabby and dated.

County School and Fire Station 1903 50283

This view looks west along Throwley Road towards the Municipal Offices. Across the High Street into Hill Road, the tower of the Baptist church is visible behind the Municipal Offices' cupola. In the foreground is the County School for Boys, which opened in 1899. All were demolished in 1971 for an exposed concrete-framed replacement, including a 14-storey office tower on the site of the school, which was, until recently, occupied by Securicor, but is apparently now empty (August 2001).

◄ **Manor Park War Memorial 1932** 85083
East of Throwley Road is Manor Park. It grew in area as a result of purchases and gifts, but started out as a war memorial park. The War Memorial itself, dedicated in June 1921, was built with the proceeds of public subscription and designed by the architect, J Burmester. Behind, Manor Park House can be seen before it was demolished in 1976. The site was used for the new Central Library.

Public Baths 1903 50284

These baths are around the corner from where Throwley Road once turned to the north (it is now Throwley Way and acts as an inner relief road or High Street by-pass). In the background is the chimney for the boiler house which was used to heat the pool water and the slipper baths. Every week I used to walk to the baths in a crocodile of schoolboys from Sutton High School for Boys in Cheam Road, for swimming lessons. The building was demolished in 1971.

Manor Park 1932 85082

This view is taken further west in the park. This curiously old-fashioned Victorian style fountain was installed in June 1931 on land acquired that year. According to a bronze plaque, the fountain was given to the town in 1925 by Councillor Charles Yates, the then Chairman of the Urban District Council,. However, it was not erected until six years later. There was also a bandstand in the park, but this became unsafe and was dismantled in the 1950s.

Cock Hotel and High Street c1955 S233029

The Cock Hotel was demolished in 1961, six years after this view was taken. Its replacement was an uninspiring office block called Old Inn House. The terrace of shops stepping down the High Street, beyond the busy junction with Carshalton Road and William Pile Ltd (the stuccoed corner building), was erected in 1880. Beyond are the cupola and turret of the Municipal Offices of 1900.

High Street c1955 S233035
This view focuses on the stuccoed corner building that was
occupied by William Pile, the bookseller and stationer. As a
schoolboy I spent many a happy hour, and much pocket
money, in the building, which was originally erected in 1883.
After 1900 it was altered and stuccoed. Before 1932 it took in
the next building down the High Street and acquired the clock
cupola. William Pile closed in 1966, but the building survived for
some years, as seen in the next view (S233104).

High Street c1965 S233104
In this view, the stuccoed corner building has just ceased to be
William Pile, the bookseller and stationer, and has become
electricity board showrooms, complete with a then-fashionable
mosaic tiled fascia. The building was demolished in 1987 and
replaced by a red brick four-storey office building, now
Lloyds TSB. The Municipal Offices have yet to go, and the distant
crane is working on the site to be occupied by Eagle Star House, a
tower block seen in view S233121, and now occupied by
Zurich Insurance.

High Street c1960 S233076

This is a view that looks north down the opposite side of the High Street. The Neo-Georgian Lloyds Bank is on the corner of Cheam Road, while beyond is an 1870 terrace, with two storeys of wide tripartite sash windows over the shops. Further down the hill is Shinner's department store, with the café restaurant sign above its cornice. The High Street is now pedestrianised and free of bus fumes. Shinner's store has also gone.

High Street c1955 S233049

This view shows the contrast between the 1870 terrace on the left and the 1880 terrace on the right. The earlier terrace is plainer with a parapet, and the later one has coved cornices to the slate roofs. There is also more decoration on the 1880 façades. The first floor windows are arched and decorated with different coloured bricks, a style known somewhat grandiosely as 'Constructional Polychromy'.

High Street c1960 S233096
This view, taken probably from the roof of the Cock Hotel, looks north downhill along the High Street. In the middle distance on the left is the large cornice and parapet of Shinner's department store. Ernest Shinner opened his first shop in 1899, and rapidly expanded to take over the whole terrace. In 1934 he bought the Baptist church at the corner of Hill Road. This he demolished and the classical façade was completed. In the 1980s it was taken over by Allders of Croydon, and then demolished in 1992.

High Street c1955 S233054
The building with flags above its cornice is Shinner's department store.
The 1930s buildings on the right have also been demolished since, and
the site is now partly occupied by Boots, a building designed in 1969
by Basil Whiting. It has a large blank upper storey and is not a great
success in townscape terms. Many of the buildings on the left have
also gone. There are entrances here into the modern Times Square
shopping centre, which fills the space behind the High Street frontages.

High Street c1965 S233121
This is a little further north, and looks towards Sutton Green with Owen Luder's 1962-67 office tower closing the vista. Three of the 1930s grand new shops can be seen. On the far right, in the foreground, are British Home Stores and Marks and Spencer, both of which are both still occupied. On the left, the Baroque-style building is now Top Shop. It had three storeys above the shops and a heavy cornice, and opened in 1931 as Fraser's ironmongery store. By 1934 it was occupied by John Perring's furniture store. The tree marks the site of the Greyhound Hotel , which can be seen in the next view (85078).

High Street 1932
85078

This delightful period view, with an Austin 7 approaching, shows the Greyhound Hotel on the right. It was one of Sutton's oldest inns, although it was rebuilt in 1873. Like the Cock, its signboard was carried on a beam across the road. This was removed in 1938. On the left is the corner of Perrin's, which is now Top Shop, and beyond is Kingham's Stores (dating from 1894) now occupied by Vision Express. The Greyhound was demolished in 1959, and replaced by a Woolworth's store, which has now also relocated. The landmark tree survived until the storms of 1987.

High Street 1894

33753

Taken further north, this austere view shows the terrace of shops built in 1893. Some well-known shop names can be seen here: including the grocers Home and Colonial and the shoe shop chain Freeman Hardy and Willis. The two shops on the left are now Bon Marche. Behind the photographer is Benhill Avenue. The last building, No 211, on the corner of Greenford Road, has since been rebuilt in an impoverished 1930s Art Deco style, and most of the buildings in the distance have also been replaced.

High Street c1960 S233077
This view is taken from the southern edge of the crossroads where High Street, Carshalton Road and Cheam Road meet. The photographer is looking from an upstairs window in the Cock Hotel down Cheam Road. The fine 1890s Barclays Bank is on the left corner, and the thinner 1920s Neo-Georgian Lloyds Bank on the right. In the distance is the superb tower of the 1907 Methodist Church, crowned by the unusual spire carried on converging flying buttresses. It is based on the 15th-century towers of St Giles Cathedral, Edinburgh, and St Nicholas Cathedral, Newcastle.

Cheam Road c1955 S233037
This view into Cheam Road, from the central crossroads of the town, is given a deceptively rural feel by the substantial trees that line the raised pavement. They hide the buildings of Sutton High School for Boys. In 1962 the site was sold for redevelopment, and after some years of desolation it was eventually occupied by Safeway supermarket, whose premises stretch as far south as Grove Road.

Cheam Road c1955 S233036
This view looks east towards the Cock Hotel and the High Street crossroads. The 1909 police station in Carshalton Road is in the distance. Behind it is the side elevation of the Congregational Church of 1888. This was demolished in 1976 to make way for the eastern inner relief road. Out of sight on the left, behind the old telephone kiosk, was the Cheam Road Cinema of 1911, a stylish and grand building whose frontage block was removed in the 1970s and replaced by a bland blank façade. It is now the night club 'Legends'.

▼ High Street 1902 48865

Although the railway station opened in 1847 some 200 yards south of the Cock Hotel crossroads, development did not really get under way here until the Epsom Downs line opened in 1865, and new station buildings were erected. This terrace of shops with accommodation above dates from about 1870, and is in an austere style with plain parapets above brick cornices. Bowling's the ironmongers moved to Grove Road in the 1920s, and their shop became a branch of the Midland Bank. This has since been converted to a pub called 'The Old Bank'.

▼ High Street c1960 S233074

This 1960s view is a taken a little further north from the station, with the entrance to Grove Road half-way along on the left. Opposite the corner building of the 1880s terrace, now painted, is Sutton Court Road. Two buildings of the 1870s terrace on the right were demolished for 1970s road widening. The painted corner building has a superb Art Nouveau stone bank façade, designed by Frederick Wheeler in 1902; it is now a pub, called The Cock and Bull.

▲ High Street c1950

S233004
Remarkably, little has changed in this view, although the Midland Bank on the right is now a pub, and the Station Hotel on the left (beyond Hall and Co, coal and coke merchants) is now part of the Litten Tree pub chain. This view captures the austere feel of the 1950s rather well, with little traffic and the 19th-century shop fronts still intact. This was the era before the blitzkrieg of 'modern' plastic fascias, which can be seen in the previous photograph, S233074.

The Station c1960 S233073 Sutton has had four station buildings. The first, built in 1847, was a small timber one, as befitted a town of only about 1500 inhabitants. The building was moved and now serves as a score-box at Sutton's cricket pitch. The second came in 1865 with the arrival of the Epsom Downs line, when Sutton became a railway junction. This was demolished in 1885. In 1928 the present one was built, as seen in this view taken during its Southern Region days.

General View c1965

S233136

This view from the upper floors of one of Sutton's new office towers, Sutherland House, looks past Station Parade to the station and the new 1960s skyline. Older church towers are to the left, and the brand new office block towers ring the north and east sides of the town centre. Tallest is that on the right - the bland, overbearing, seventeen storeys of Vigilant House. It was started in 1961, then refurbished during the 1990s and renamed South Point.

◀ **Grove Road c1960**
S233075
This view looks east towards the High Street, past the Post Office on the right. The brick buildings at the far end, their six windows facing the camera, were demolished in the 1970s for the widening of Sutton Court Road. The cars in the centre of Grove Road have long gone; this road is now a busy and key part of the town centre ring road system.

Grove Road c1950 S233009

Grove Road runs westwards from the High Street, parallel to the railway line. It was laid out in Victorian times, and was tree-lined throughout its length. By the 1950s however, the trees had been removed at the High Street end, but in the distance they still remain, lining the residential section of Grove Road as it heads towards Cheam. On the left is the pedimented Masonic Hall, with the 1929 Telephone Exchange next door. This has since been heightened by two storeys. The old Post Office beyond has also been rebuilt.

Mulgrave Road c1955

S233033

On the left, the three-storey neo-Georgian shops (with flats over) of Mulgrave Court were built in 1931. The single-storey shops beyond have since had an upper storey added. Today the 17-storey South Point would dominate this scene. The centre of Mulgrave Road still has its taxi rank, albeit with more modern cabs.

Brighton Road c1960 S233069

Descending southwards, High Street becomes Brighton Road. It is flanked by blocks of flats with shops on their ground floors. On the left, the 1930s shops are called Regent Parade, while the flats above are Grosvenor Court. On the right, behind the trees, is Tudor Court, a further range of flats over shops, this time with mock timber framing of a Tudor character. These types of developments were ideally situated for railway commuters, and they set a trend which was enthusiastically taken up elsewhere. In Sutton there are now vast numbers of blocks of flats dating from the 1960s onwards.

The Green 1898 41713
This view shows the pond in its heyday, and looks south-east towards the High Street buildings of the 1870s which are to the right of the island. On the left is the Cricketers pub. This building dates partly from 1790, but has later extensions. It is now rather irritatingly renamed the Fielder and Firkin. The pond was known as Victoria Pond - the weeping willow on the island was planted in 1838 to commemorate Queen Victoria's coronation. An elm was planted in 1898 for her Diamond Jubilee. In 1955 the pond was filled in, and is now only a memory.

The Green and Benhilton

◀ **The Green 1894** 34062
The road to London passes
through The Green, which was
preserved by the 1810 Act of
Parliament that enclosed the rest of
the former common land of the
parish for agriculture. It is an
attractive open area, and this view
looks north past the pond across
Bushey Road, with the row of elms
on the right. The pond was
notorious for its summer stinks,
and in 1894 the new concrete base
and sidewalls were completed.

◀ **The Green 1898** 41712
This view, taken in the
same year as 41713,
looks northwards from
beside the north bank of
the pond. It shows
newly-planted bushes
and trees, which can be
seen in a more mature
state in view 85084. The
elm trees lasted until the
1970s when an
epidemic of Dutch elm
disease killed them. In
the distance, on the left,
is Elmsleigh, a fine
house of the 1860s,
now demolished.

The Green 1932 85084

By 1932 the elms along the east side of the Green have been polled, but their trunks are stouter and more mature. In the distance is the elaborate drinking fountain built in 1902 in green faience. This was Sutton's contribution to the national celebrations for the coronation of King Edward VII. Beyond the trees on the right, behind the Camp coffee advert, are the tea rooms, which were built in 1896. They are now occupied by the Jade Palace Chinese restaurant.

Benhilton Church 1904 51191

This church is superbly situated on a ridge of high ground, making it visible for miles around. It was designed in a convincingly medieval style by the noted architect Samuel Teulon in 1865. One would be forgiven for thinking this fine church was the parish church for Sutton, but it is not - it served the new parish of north Sutton and the new Victorian suburb of Benhilton. This view is along the path from Angel Hill, which still remains a footpath.

Benhilton, All Saints Church c1955 B67002

This view is taken from the west, near the north-east corner of the Green, at the foot of Angel Hill. The fine west tower of All Saints dominates the scene. The chancel east window was blown out by bomb blasts in 1944, and the vicarage severely damaged. The Victorian school also suffered a direct hit and was totally destroyed, but nothing in this view was affected.

◄ **The Footbridge, Angel Hill c1955** S233022
By 1937 the old bridge had become dangerous and was removed. It was replaced by a temporary steel structure, which itself was hit by German bombs in September 1940. A second steel girder bridge, also intended to be temporary and seen here, survived until about 1980, when the present concrete span, which is carried on imitation rubble stone abutments, was erected.

◄ **Benhilton Bridge 1894** 34064
The main road from London
originally climbed Angel Hill's
ridge, but in the early 19th
century a cutting was made.
According to local legend this was
created at the order of the Prince
Regent, who used the London to
Brighton road to travel to his
Pavilion by the sea at Brighton.
Other sources say the cutting was
made in the 1770s as part of the
turnpiking of the main road.
Whichever version is true, the
cutting remains at its original
width, and this view shows the
rather elegant Victorian footbridge
that crosses the main road.

▼ **The Angel 1896** 38926
At the top of Angel Hill is the
Angel Inn, an early 19th-
century building. It was once a
stop where coaches and
travellers changed horses
before the descent into Sutton.
In 1896 it was still used as
livery stables. The main
changes to the scene made
since the picture was taken are
the removal of the signboard
at the left, and the unfortunate
roughcasting and painting of
the brickwork. Needless to say
no livery facility is necessary in
the age of the motorcar.

◄ **Benhill Road 1903** 50287
The next four photographs
show the well-to-do suburb of
Benhilton - served by the
church of All Saints, built in
1865. The church tower can
be seen in the centre of the
view, which looks west along
what is now called All Saints
Road (in 1903 it was Benhill
Road). The road is much
changed with blocks of flats
along the left side and semi-
detached houses on the right.
A commemorative plaque
informs passers-by that these
were built in 1958 by A J R
Richards.

Benhill Wood Road 1904 51190
Benhill Wood Road runs south-east from All Saints Road, and once
went through Benhill Woods. It was laid out in the 1860s, and had
numerous large houses which were occupied by prosperous citizens
of Sutton. These have nearly all fallen victim to the modern developer
and the obsession in Sutton with replacing large houses with blocks of
flats. As a consequence, the appearance of the road is much changed.

Benhilton, The Hilton 1904 51193
This building is typical of the grand villas that were built along Benhill Wood Road. The Hilton is a name that nowadays evokes standardised luxury hotels. It was built in the 1870s, and is visible behind the trees in view 51190. The Hilton is typical of the good quality design used in the Benhilton area of Sutton, and features window blind boxes and an attached conservatory with plants and shrubs. As in so many other cases, the site is now occupied by modern housing.

Woodside House School 1898 41715
This is another of Benhilton's 1870 villas in attractive wooded grounds. By 1898 Woodside House, in Woodside Road, had become a small private school. Note the round-arched windows and the ornamental bargeboards that are characteristic of the 1860s and early 1870s. Woodside Road was also laid through the former Benhill Woods. Some of the larger trees in the gardens survived, although most are now in the grounds of the blocks of flats that replaced many of the Victorian villas.

Parish Church 1894 34059 ▶

As befitted a growing Victorian town, the spiritual needs of the new citizens were vigorously addressed. Where once there were just a single crumbling, partly medieval, parish church and a small Wesleyan Chapel built in 1841, numerous churches of numerous Christian denominations soon sprang up. We have already seen All Saints in Benhilton, and this view shows the old parish church of St Nicholas, which did not escape the church building fervour - it was entirely rebuilt in the 1860s.

◀ **St Nicholas Church 1932** 85081

The old church had a medieval nave and chancel, and its brick west tower, built around 1800, replaced a medieval timber bell tower. The new church was designed by Edwin Nash, and opened in 1864. It is a rather uninspiring essay in the Decorated Gothic style, built in hard flints with stone dressings. Its tower is crowned by a broach spire. It is well worth a visit though, for the superb monuments have been taken from the old church, and re-erected in the new one. This includes one by William Stanton to Lady Brownlow of about 1700, although it is somewhat obscured by the organ.

Victorian and Later Sutton: Churches and Suburbs

Wesleyan Chapel 1894 ▶

33757

The chapel was built in 1884 on the south side of Carshalton Road, but has since been demolished. After 1907, when the new church was built in Cheam Road, it ceased to be a church and bizarrely became the Sutton Hippodrome cinema. Later it became engineering workshops, before being demolished in the 1950s.

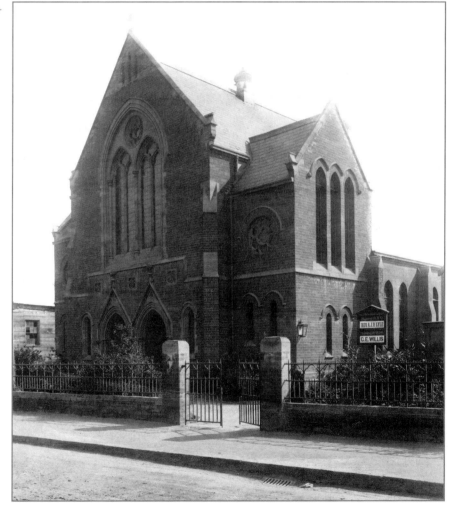

◄ **Congregational Church 1894** 34060
The Congregational Church stood to the east of the police station on the south side of Carshalton Road, until it was demolished in 1976 as part of a scheme of road improvements. The site is now part of Chalk Pit Way on the inner ring road. It was built in 1888, with the façade facing the road constructed to the highest standards in ragstone with stone dressings.

Wesleyan Church 1913 65223

The new Wesleyan Church, seen here from Church Road (now St Nicholas Way), was a sumptuous and unusual building. It is distinguished by its fine tower and spire, which is based on the 'crown' of the medieval St Giles Cathedral, Edinburgh. The spire is carried on four converging flying buttresses. Cheam Road is to the right and the church hall, Trinity Hall, is on the left. It was designed by Gordon and Gunton and built in 1907. It is considered by many to be one of Sutton's most interesting surviving buildings. It is now shared by the Methodists and the United Reformed Church.

St Barnabas Church 1904

52974

St Barnabas Church was built in the 1880s to the designs of Carpenter and Ingelow. It served the Sutton New Town development to the east of Manor Park up to the Carshalton parish boundary. The road is now St Barnabas Road. The church, on the west side of the road, is built in brick with a polygonal bell tower. There is a modern vicarage to the right, but the boundary wall, railings and gate piers have all survived.

Benhilton Road 1903 50286

This view is taken from the junction with Carshalton Road, south from St Barnabas Church. As we look north down St Barnabas Road, we see that the trees and houses look very new. On the right is the Roman Catholic Church of Our Lady of the Rosary, which was converted from a school in 1887 by E Ingress Bell. It is a rather undistinguished building. A porch has been added outside the double doorway, and a church hall has been built in the foreground.

▼ **The Quarry 1890** 27422

To the east of the High Street there were several chalk pits: this was the biggest. It lies to the south of Carshalton Road, and east of the Congregational Church. The famous Len's specialist railway book and model shop was situated here in a ramshackle building, precariously poised above the pit. It was one of my frequent haunts in school lunch hours. The site is now infilled, and a B & Q warehouse is currently under construction (August 2001).

▼ **Manor Park Road 1903** 50285

Manor Park Road runs along the east side of Manor Park. This view is taken a little way north of its junction with Carshalton Road. The road is much changed now, but of considerable interest is the way the road focuses on the distant tower of All Saints, Benhilton, high on its ridge, and nearly a mile to the north.

▲ **Cheam Road 1903** 49175

Here we move back to the west of the High Street. This view looks along Cheam Road, with the Cheam Road Hall on the right. This building is now dominated by the Methodist Church, which was built four years after this photograph was taken. Sadly the trees have gone, along with the house on the far left, which was part of Sutton High School for Boys.

◀ High School for Girls 1904

51194

This view is also of the south side of the road, but further west. Sutton High School for Girls still thrives today. It was founded in 1883, and opened in January 1884 with eighty girls and eight teachers. The school has expanded greatly, and is a key member of the Girls Public Day School Trust. The building bears a sign dating it to the1880s (the last number is, unfortunately, indecipherable). To its right is the original house, Park House, which the school leased after it came on the market.

Cheam Road 1903 50292

The photographer has moved further west along Cheam Road, and is now looking eastwards back towards the town centre. The footpaths are still raised above the level of the roadway and there are substantial trees on the left. Unfortunately, these were elms, and succumbed to Dutch elm disease and road improvement schemes.

Church Road 1904 51184

This view looks north along Church Road from near the Cheam Road junction, with the spire of St Nicholas parish church in the distance. The road is now called St Nicholas Way, and forms part of the town's inner ring road or gyratory. The houses on the left have been replaced by Civic Offices and the Central Library, which opened in 1978. On the right, three years after the date of this photograph, the Methodist Church was built.

Gander Green Lane 1903 50295
This is a delightfully rural Edwardian view, which looks north along Gander Green Lane, from near the junction with Cheam Road. This scene is, needless to say, much changed, but behind the trees on the right the ground remains undeveloped. In 1828 the old chalk pits were infilled with the excavations from the railway cutting near West Sutton station, which extended the grounds of Sutton Cricket Club. The fence on the left belonged to the grounds of Lower Cheam House, which was built around 1800, but demolished for housing in 1933. The parish boundary between Sutton and Cheam follows much of Gander Green Lane.

Worcester Road 1913 65222
This view looks east from Cornwall Road along Worcester Road towards the town centre. This was another desirable residential road, with prosperous Victorian villas at its eastern end. Edwardian and later houses can be seen in the foreground, including Dumbreck House on the left hand corner. This house was built in the Arts and Crafts style around 1910. As is the case with Mulgrave Road, a few modern blocks of flats replace the earlier houses.

Mulgrave Road 1913 65221

The next sequence of views shows the Victorian and later development of Sutton to the south of the railway line. We begin with Mulgrave Road, which started as shops and flats, but soon became entirely residential. The road runs south and parallel to the railway as far west as Belmont Rise. In this view the photographer is looking east past the junction with Cornwall Road, with the Edwardian houses numbered 152 and 150 nearest to the camera on the left. At this end of the road the houses have been spared demolition by developers, and have not been replaced by blocks of flats.

Grange Vale 1904 52975

The Epsom Downs railway line was opened in 1865, and branched south from Sutton station to its first stop, which was Belmont. This view looks east, and shows the bridge across Grange Vale, a road that connects the Brighton Road with the residential areas of Grange Road, Worcester Road and Mulgrave Road. Since the photograph was taken, houses have been built to the right, and a block of flats to the left. The bridge now has a metal mesh balustrade, but the cast-iron spans are unchanged.

Cavendish Road 1903 49177

The next views are of the residential roads laid out to the east of Brighton Road. Cavendish Road, which runs from Brighton Road east to Langley Park Road, is a good example of the earlier phases of suburban growth in Sutton. Its development in the early 1870s was facilitated by the Sutton Water Company, which was founded in 1864. Their deep boreholes could be used to pump piped water to the neighbourhood, without the need for individual house wells, which were not a practical proposition on the chalk plateau.

Cavendish Road 1903
49178
These fine semi-
detached villas date
from the early 1870s
and make excellent
homes. Sadly, almost all
of those on the south
side of the road have
been demolished, and
have been replaced by
buildings characteristic
of the town's expansion
during the second half
of the 20th century:
three storey blocks of
flats. Fortunately,
several of the Victorian
houses survive on the
north side (house
number 1 and numbers
7 to 33 remain), and
thus Cavendish Road at
least retains some of its
character.

◀ **Christchurch Park 1903**
49180
The next three Edwardian views show Christchurch Park, which was the southern limit of development at that date. The views are remarkably evocative of a past era of the town, as the road has, with one notable exception, been entirely redeveloped. The replacement buildings are, without exception, blocks of flats, mostly three-storey, built between the 1950s and the present day.

Langley Park Road 1903

49179

Roads like the one shown here have fared less well. In this view, looking south just past the junction of Cavendish Road and Albion Road, the two large houses on the left remain, but flats and a close of small modern houses, Milestone Close, have replaced the rest. These large houses were packed closely together, unlike in the more prosperous neighbourhood of Benhilton, which is to the north of the railway.

Christchurch Park 1903

49182

View 49180 looks west from the junction with Langley Park Road along Christchurch Park, with the well-known copper beech trees newly planted in the verges. This view, however, looks northwards from fields. These have long since been built over, and were situated where Devonshire Avenue is now. All these houses have now gone, to be replaced by blocks of flats.

Christchurch Park 1903

49181

Christchurch Park was laid out as a road in 1888, converting a track through fields into a prosperous residential area. The only surviving building from the Christchurch Park development is its great red brick church, Christ Church, designed in 1888 by Newman and Jacques. It has no tower, but its scale was such that it dominated all around it (at least until the flat blocks arrived).

◀ **The Ridgeway 1913** 65218
Over the parish boundary in
Carshalton in what was named
Carshalton Beeches, lavender fields
were developed in the years after
after 1905. Lavender had been
grown for the distilleries in Mitcham.
The plant was cut when in flower,
and crushed in mills to extract its oils
for the perfume industry - hence the
name 'Mitcham Lavender'. The
Ridgeway is one of the roads that
was laid out to replace these
lavender fields. The area is known as
the Highfields Estate, and its
popularity was assured when
Carshalton Beeches station opened
in 1907.

◀ Albion Road 1904 52977
Albion Road, the most easterly of the Victorian developments south of the railway, has its back garden fences along the parish boundary with Carshalton. Here the photographer is looking east from the junction with Langley Park Road. There are substantial houses with large dormers on the right, some of which still remain. The left hand villa in the distance has succumbed, but the one beside it, partly screened by trees, still survives as a substantial family house.

▼ South Metropolitan District Schools 1896 38943
These imposing Victorian buildings were constructed in 1853 and extended in 1871. They were the South Metropolitan District Schools, where over 1,500 pauper children from south London were sent, as well as any vagrant children spotted by the authorities. The school closed in 1902 and had a variety of uses, including acting as a workhouse. Finally it became an industrial neurosis unit and psychiatric hospital, before being demolished in 1982. It was replaced by a housing estate, Belmont Heights, with access across the railway line from the Brighton Road, north of Belmont Station.

◀ Golf Links 1903 50299
This scene is of Banstead Downs, which are actually outside Sutton's boundaries, south of Belmont station. The clubhouse of the Banstead Downs Golf Club is seen in the distance. Between the golfers and the clubhouse was Burdon Lane, which until the 1950s joined the Brighton Road as it crossed the Downs by way of a dangerous blind junction. However, this stretch was later closed and became a path, so that golfers today no longer have to cross a road to get to their clubhouse.

◀ **Worcester Park
Central Road c1955** W455043
Worcester Park is situated north-west of Sutton along Malden Road. Until the railway arrived in 1859 the area was predominantly agricultural, with only a few farmhouses and cottages. This is a view of Central Road, originally called Cheam Common Hill. This area was extensively rebuilt in the 1930s, when a tide of semi-detached housing swept across the fields. The buildings on the right, Caldbeck Parade, were built in 1932, while on the left is the Odeon, which was built in 1936 and demolished in the 1990s.

The Suburbs to the North and Northwest

◄ **Cheam**
Railway Bridge 1904 51198
The tour briefly visits Cheam; this view looks south through the railway bridge on Station Way, the station fencing being visible on the left. The railway station opened in 1847, and the bridge dates from that time. However, it was doubled in width in 1907, by way of a flat steel decked bridge which largely obscures the original construction. The building on the left is the old smithy. Built in 1860, it closed in about 1928 and is now a house, The Old Forge.

◄ **Worcester Park**
The Pond c1955 W455036
Continuing along Malden Road we reach the junction with Church Road. This leads to St John's Church, Old Malden, which dates partly from medieval times and partly from the early 17th century. These old sections were later incorporated into the south aisle of a much larger Victorian church. At the junction, however, the character is wholly suburban. Out of shot, to the right, is the Plough pub. The pond in front of it has since been filled in. On the opposite side of Malden Road are typical suburban shopping parades, which are still here today.

**New Malden
High Street c1960**

N167062

Crossing the A3 Kingston By-pass, Malden Road soon becomes New Malden's High Street. This suburb matured when the railway arrived, and the street accumulated a typical suburban melange of architectural styles. 1921 neo-Georgian can be seen on the right in the middle distance, and beyond there is a long terrace of late 19th-century buildings with terra cotta bay windows. On the left, mock timber-frames and gables jostle with late 1950s and late Victorian styles. This view is now obstructed by two sixteen-storey office tower blocks, which were built in the mid 1960s.

◀ **Raynes Park
Grand Drive c1950** R355003
Beyond Raynes Park station
we turn south, and head along
Grand Avenue to the junction
with Cannon Hill Lane. Here
the semi-detached houses
seen in the distance give way
to a block of 1930s Neo-
Georgian flats called Thornton
Court. Across Cannon Hill
Lane the long neo-Georgian
shopping parade is visible. The
fields behind the chain link
fence are now occupied by
school buildings, and opposite
the shops is St John Fisher
Roman Catholic Primary
School.

Raynes Park c1955
R355006

The architecture of Raynes Park is in general suburban and undistinguished. This view looks northwest along Coombe Lane, with a bus turning left into West Barnes Lane. On the right are 1930s and 1950s shopping parades. The concrete plank fence on the left is still here, and screens a Thames Water depot.

Stonecot Hill c1955 S233050

Continuing from Grand Drive into Tudor Drive the route briefly re-enters the parish of Sutton at Stonecot Hill. This follows the course of the old Roman road from London to Chichester, called Stane Street, which is nowadays the busy A24 road from London to Worthing. On the left traffic waits to cross the junction of Stonecot Hill with Sutton Common Road. The Stonecot Garage has been rebuilt since the time of this picture and is now a Shell petrol station. In the parade of shops Frederick W Paine, the undertaker, is still in business, although his trademark showing an oversized lantern has gone, leaving just its bracket.

Stonecot Hill c1955
S233057

This view, taken from Stonecot Hill, shows the 1930s Woodstock pub, which still flourishes. It is now different in appearance, as most of the ground floor has been painted, including the right hand bay window. One brick gate pier is still intact, although without the lamp.

Morden
Looking West c1965
M359055
Further northeast along Stane Street (or the A24), we reach Morden. This aerial view is taken from the 14-storey curved office block of Crown House, which was built in 1960. Here we look south-east along London Road, with the Northern Line tube depot and train sheds to the left. Between the road and the railway are terraces of white painted Art Deco 1930s shops and flats, called Morden Court. The mock Tudor of York Close can be seen to the left, and some of Victorian Morden is visible on the right.

Mitcham
Lower Green c1960
M296092

Mitcham is a town with two greens. This view is of Lower Green, and on the right, out of view, is Cricket Green. In the middle of the green is the Vestry Hall, built in 1887, which has a cupola and clock tower. Around Cricket Green and along Church Road are some good late 18th- and early 19th-century houses. To the south-east is Mitcham Common, which offers more open space and increased rural character.

◄ **Morden**
Crown Lane c1960 M359020
Back at ground level, the photographer is looking east along Crown Lane. The 1990s Civic Centre is now on the right, behind the bus stop. The scene is now dominated by the 14 storeys of Crown House. Victoria Buildings on the left curve away towards Frank Holden's 1926 Morden tube station. The block in the distance, along Aberconway Road, is dated 1936, while the Odeon has been demolished, its site now occupied by Iceland frozen food shop.

▼ **Mitcham**
Upper Green c1955 M296032
Upper Green is further northeast, and like Lower Green suffers from traffic. However, the two roads in the foreground are now traffic-free footpaths and something of an improvement. The gasholder in the distance is still there, as are the buildings, including the King's Arms on the far right, which was built in 1906. I have happy memories of attending jazz and rhythm and blues clubs there as a teenager in the 1960s, which took place in an upstairs room.

◄ **Carshalton**
St Helier, Bishopsford Road c1955 C38020
Heading back south this brief tour passes through Rose Hill. The St Helier Estate was built to rehouse Londoners by the London County Council between 1928 and 1936 on farmland north of Sutton. A vast council estate of over 9,000 houses and flats, mostly in Neo-Georgian style, replaced the old lavender fields. An exception was Rose Hill Court. The flats over the shops were built in Art Deco or 'Ocean Liner' style. These are at the junction of St Helier Avenue and Bishopsford Road. The Gaumont cinema is now the Mecca Bingo.

Carshalton
St Helier Hospital c1965 C38046

The vast St Helier Hospital was built to serve the St Helier Estate. It is situated to the south-east of the Rose Hill Roundabout. This white painted Moderne style complex dates from 1938, and is little altered today apart from some low key extensions. It dominates the rows of neo-Georgian council houses that surround it, many of which are now privately owned. Some can be seen in this aerial view. The scruffy open space to the left is now the much neater St Helier Open Space, with the Carshalton Arena out of view to the left. In the foreground Greenshaw Woods and Rosehill Park East can be seen.

A Tour to the East

Carshalton
High Street 1896 37667
The second brief tour starts in Carshalton, where I lived as a
teenager. This view shows the High Street with the King's Arms
on the left. This has now gone and has been replaced by 1950s
shops - I used to collect the family bread from one every
Saturday morning. The building in the distance is the Coach and
Horses, which is still a pub today, and behind it is the parish
church, which was much enlarged in the 1890s.

◀ **Carshalton**
Benyon Road c1955 C38003
This view is taken looking north-west along Benyon Road towards the junction of Pound Street and Carshalton Road. The high brick wall in the distance belongs to Carshalton House. This was the village's grandest house, a mansion designed by Giacomo Leoni in the early 18th century for Edward Carlton, who was a London tobacco merchant. Its fine landscaped grounds with a lake include the important garden buildings, the Hermitage and the Water House, now part of a school. St Philomena's Convent School was founded in 1893 by the Daughters of the Cross.

◄ Carshalton
Pond from the Bridge 1896 37669
Carshalton's ponds, which are spring-fed and lead to the River Wandle, are a most attractive feature in the centre of the village. Further lakes and streams flow through the grounds of The Grove, which was once a private house, but is now a delightful public park. In this view looking south-west from Honeywood Walk to Pound Street, we see the Greyhound pub, which is part 18th-century and part 19th-century Jacobean. On the right is Honeywood House, seen before it was extended in 1903. It is now the London Borough of Sutton's Heritage Centre.

▼ Carshalton
The Bridge 1895 35148
The railway from Mitcham Junction to Sutton crosses Mill Lane and the river Wandle over this fine bridge. Through the railway bridge the single low arch of the brick Butter Hill road bridge can be seen. Behind is Ansell's Snuff Mill, a late 18th-century building, which is now demolished. The Wandle is now narrower, with a lower flow than in 1895.

◄ Hackbridge
The Old Red Lion c1955 H425005
Further north, along Nightingale Road, the road crosses the Wandle to become Hackbridge Road. Just past Hackbridge Green is one of the hamlet's oldest buildings, the early 18th-century Red Lion pub. In the foreground is the corner of The Green, and in the distance, to the left of the pub, the five-light dormer window belongs to Hackbridge Infants School.

Hackbridge, The Triangle c1955 H425007
At the junction of Hackbridge Road and London Road is the area called The Triangle. The buildings are mostly early 20th-century and 1930s shopping parades. The south corner is occupied by Hackbridge Junior School (in the foreground), with the Infants School beyond. Both were built in 1901, and celebrate their centenary this year (2001).

Hackbridge, The Triangle c1955 H425006
Here the photographer looks north from the southern part of The Triangle. The Hackbridge Road junction is on the left, and the tree, now gone, is in the waste ground between Hackbridge Junior School and the road. The shopping parade on the right is in a competent neo-Georgian style, with box sash windows and a brick dentilled cornice to the parapet, and a centrepiece triangular pediment. The opposite parade is considerably less architecturally distinguished.

Beddington
On The Wandle 1894 34376

This view of the tranquil River Wandle, with children playing at its edge, belies the river's industrial importance. Here the photographer looks towards a mill owner's house with stone mill wheels leaning against the wall. The Wandle is only nine miles long, and has Young's Wandworth Brewery at its mouth, and numerous mills along its length, many in Beddington Corner, Hackbridge and Carshalton. Later many of the mills were replaced by vinyl and plastics works, which themselves have now gone, but whose smells were notorious in north Carshalton in the 1960s.

Beddington
The Sports Field c1960
B50029

To the east of Beddington Park and the historic Carew Manor we reach Plough Lane and turn south to cross the railway bridge. Here the photographer looks north-east from the railway bridge across a sports field. The cricket square is preserved amid derelict scrubland, but trees now obscure the view. Beyond the houses in Bristow Road are the giant cooling towers and chimneys of Croydon Power Station. These have now all gone, apart from the two chimneys, which are part of an Ikea store.

**Wallington
The Green 1903** 49189
The hamlet of Wallington grew up around the Green before Victorian expansion headed south, when the railway arrived up the hill. The Duke's Head on the left was rebuilt about 1830, and the arched windowed wing fronting Manor Road was added around 1850. Behind are several Regency stucco houses, while opposite are shops with flats over, built about 1870. The trees were removed around 1970, and in the early 1980s offices replaced the building on the left. Even now the Green still retains its character.

Wallington, Malden Road 1903 49186

After the railway arrived in 1847 development soon followed, and Wallington became a separate parish in 1867. Immediately, a parish church, Holy Trinity, was built. This was situated halfway between the old village centre around The Green, and the new development around the station. Here the photographer looks west along Maldon road towards Manor Road, with Holy Trinity at the junction. The church was designed by Habershon and Brock, and was completed in 1867. It is the church in which I was confirmed in 1965. The houses on the right have long given way to blocks of flats.

Wallington, Woodcote Road c1950 W11007

This view looks north along Woodcote Road towards the railway bridge. The station is on the left, but is concealed by the distant shops. This is the commercial heart of Victorian Wallington, uphill from The Green, and we see a fine row of Edwardian shops with flats above. Their canted full-height bay windows step down the hill in an elegant rhythm. Unfortunately, the developments on the left are considerably less consistent, being built at various times between 1910 and the 1950s.

Index

Frith Book Co Titles

www.francisfrith.co.uk

The Frith Book Company publishes over 100 new titles each year. A selection of those currently available are listed below. For latest catalogue please contact Frith Book Co.

Town Books 96 pages, approx 100 photos. County and Themed Books 128 pages, approx 150 photos (unless specified). All titles hardback laminated case and jacket except those indicated pb (paperback)

Amersham, Chesham & Rickmansworth (pb)			Derby (pb)	1-85937-367-4	£9.99
	1-85937-340-2	£9.99	Derbyshire (pb)	1-85937-196-5	£9.99
Ancient Monuments & Stone Circles	1-85937-143-4	£17.99	Devon (pb)	1-85937-297-x	£9.99
Aylesbury (pb)	1-85937-227-9	£9.99	Dorset (pb)	1-85937-269-4	£9.99
Bakewell	1-85937-113-2	£12.99	Dorset Churches	1-85937-172-8	£17.99
Barnstaple (pb)	1-85937-300-3	£9.99	Dorset Coast (pb)	1-85937-299-6	£9.99
Bath (pb)	1-85937419-0	£9.99	Dorset Living Memories	1-85937-210-4	£14.99
Bedford (pb)	1-85937-205-8	£9.99	Down the Severn	1-85937-118-3	£14.99
Berkshire (pb)	1-85937-191-4	£9.99	Down the Thames (pb)	1-85937-278-3	£9.99
Berkshire Churches	1-85937-170-1	£17.99	Down the Trent	1-85937-311-9	£14.99
Blackpool (pb)	1-85937-382-8	£9.99	Dublin (pb)	1-85937-231-7	£9.99
Bognor Regis (pb)	1-85937-431-x	£9.99	East Anglia (pb)	1-85937-265-1	£9.99
Bournemouth	1-85937-067-5	£12.99	East London	1-85937-080-2	£14.99
Bradford (pb)	1-85937-204-x	£9.99	East Sussex	1-85937-130-2	£14.99
Brighton & Hove(pb)	1-85937-192-2	£8.99	Eastbourne	1-85937-061-6	£12.99
Bristol (pb)	1-85937-264-3	£9.99	Edinburgh (pb)	1-85937-193-0	£8.99
British Life A Century Ago (pb)	1-85937-213-9	£9.99	England in the 1880s	1-85937-331-3	£17.99
Buckinghamshire (pb)	1-85937-200-7	£9.99	English Castles (pb)	1-85937-434-4	£9.99
Camberley (pb)	1-85937-222-8	£9.99	English Country Houses	1-85937-161-2	£17.99
Cambridge (pb)	1-85937-422-0	£9.99	Essex (pb)	1-85937-270-8	£9.99
Cambridgeshire (pb)	1-85937-420-4	£9.99	Exeter	1-85937-126-4	£12.99
Canals & Waterways (pb)	1-85937-291-0	£9.99	Exmoor	1-85937-132-9	£14.99
Canterbury Cathedral (pb)	1-85937-179-5	£9.99	Falmouth	1-85937-066-7	£12.99
Cardiff (pb)	1-85937-093-4	£9.99	Folkestone (pb)	1-85937-124-8	£9.99
Carmarthenshire	1-85937-216-3	£14.99	Glasgow (pb)	1-85937-190-6	£9.99
Chelmsford (pb)	1-85937-310-0	£9.99	Gloucestershire	1-85937-102-7	£14.99
Cheltenham (pb)	1-85937-095-0	£9.99	Great Yarmouth (pb)	1-85937-426-3	£9.99
Cheshire (pb)	1-85937-271-6	£9.99	Greater Manchester (pb)	1-85937-266-x	£9.99
Chester	1-85937-090-x	£12.99	Guildford (pb)	1-85937-410-7	£9.99
Chesterfield	1-85937-378-x	£9.99	Hampshire (pb)	1-85937-279-1	£9.99
Chichester (pb)	1-85937-228-7	£9.99	Hampshire Churches (pb)	1-85937-207-4	£9.99
Colchester (pb)	1-85937-188-4	£8.99	Harrogate	1-85937-423-9	£9.99
Cornish Coast	1-85937-163-9	£14.99	Hastings & Bexhill (pb)	1-85937-131-0	£9.99
Cornwall (pb)	1-85937-229-5	£9.99	Heart of Lancashire (pb)	1-85937-197-3	£9.99
Cornwall Living Memories	1-85937-248-1	£14.99	Helston (pb)	1-85937-214-7	£9.99
Cotswolds (pb)	1-85937-230-9	£9.99	Hereford (pb)	1-85937-175-2	£9.99
Cotswolds Living Memories	1-85937-255-4	£14.99	Herefordshire	1-85937-174-4	£14.99
County Durham	1-85937-123-x	£14.99	Hertfordshire (pb)	1-85937-247-3	£9.99
Croydon Living Memories	1-85937-162-0	£9.99	Horsham (pb)	1-85937-432-8	£9.99
Cumbria	1-85937-101-9	£14.99	Humberside	1-85937-215-5	£14.99
Dartmoor	1-85937-145-0	£14.99	Hythe, Romney Marsh & Ashford	1-85937-256-2	£9.99

Available from your local bookshop or from the publisher

Ipswich (pb)	1-85937-424-7	£9.99	St Ives (pb)	1-85937415-8	£9.99
Ireland (pb)	1-85937-181-7	£9.99	Scotland (pb)	1-85937-182-5	£9.99
Isle of Man (pb)	1-85937-268-6	£9.99	Scottish Castles (pb)	1-85937-323-2	£9.99
Isles of Scilly	1-85937-136-1	£14.99	Sevenoaks & Tunbridge	1-85937-057-8	£12.99
Isle of Wight (pb)	1-85937-429-8	£9.99	Sheffield, South Yorks (pb)	1-85937-267-8	£9.99
Isle of Wight Living Memories	1-85937-304-6	£14.99	Shrewsbury (pb)	1-85937-325-9	£9.99
Kent (pb)	1-85937-189-2	£9.99	Shropshire (pb)	1-85937-326-7	£9.99
Kent Living Memories	1-85937-125-6	£14.99	Somerset	1-85937-153-1	£14.99
Lake District (pb)	1-85937-275-9	£9.99	South Devon Coast	1-85937-107-8	£14.99
Lancaster, Morecambe & Heysham (pb)	1-85937-233-3	£9.99	South Devon Living Memories	1-85937-168-x	£14.99
Leeds (pb)	1-85937-202-3	£9.99	South Hams	1-85937-220-1	£14.99
Leicester	1-85937-073-x	£12.99	Southampton (pb)	1-85937-427-1	£9.99
Leicestershire (pb)	1-85937-185-x	£9.99	Southport (pb)	1-85937-425-5	£9.99
Lincolnshire (pb)	1-85937-433-6	£9.99	Staffordshire	1-85937-047-0	£12.99
Liverpool & Merseyside (pb)	1-85937-234-1	£9.99	Stratford upon Avon	1-85937-098-5	£12.99
London (pb)	1-85937-183-3	£9.99	Suffolk (pb)	1-85937-221-x	£9.99
Ludlow (pb)	1-85937-176-0	£9.99	Suffolk Coast	1-85937-259-7	£14.99
Luton (pb)	1-85937-235-x	£9.99	Surrey (pb)	1-85937-240-6	£9.99
Maidstone	1-85937-056-x	£14.99	Sussex (pb)	1-85937-184-1	£9.99
Manchester (pb)	1-85937-198-1	£9.99	Swansea (pb)	1-85937-167-1	£9.99
Middlesex	1-85937-158-2	£14.99	Tees Valley & Cleveland	1-85937-211-2	£14.99
New Forest	1-85937-128-0	£14.99	Thanet (pb)	1-85937-116-7	£9.99
Newark (pb)	1-85937-366-6	£9.99	Tiverton (pb)	1-85937-178-7	£9.99
Newport, Wales (pb)	1-85937-258-9	£9.99	Torbay	1-85937-063-2	£12.99
Newquay (pb)	1-85937-421-2	£9.99	Truro	1-85937-147-7	£12.99
Norfolk (pb)	1-85937-195-7	£9.99	Victorian and Edwardian Cornwall	1-85937-252-x	£14.99
Norfolk Living Memories	1-85937-217-1	£14.99	Victorian & Edwardian Devon	1-85937-253-8	£14.99
Northamptonshire	1-85937-150-7	£14.99	Victorian & Edwardian Kent	1-85937-149-3	£14.99
Northumberland Tyne & Wear (pb)	1-85937-281-3	£9.99	Vic & Ed Maritime Album	1-85937-144-2	£17.99
North Devon Coast	1-85937-146-9	£14.99	Victorian and Edwardian Sussex	1-85937-157-4	£14.99
North Devon Living Memories	1-85937-261-9	£14.99	Victorian & Edwardian Yorkshire	1-85937-154-x	£14.99
North London	1-85937-206-6	£14.99	Victorian Seaside	1-85937-159-0	£17.99
North Wales (pb)	1-85937-298-8	£9.99	Villages of Devon (pb)	1-85937-293-7	£9.99
North Yorkshire (pb)	1-85937-236-8	£9.99	Villages of Kent (pb)	1-85937-294-5	£9.99
Norwich (pb)	1-85937-194-9	£8.99	Villages of Sussex (pb)	1-85937-295-3	£9.99
Nottingham (pb)	1-85937-324-0	£9.99	Warwickshire (pb)	1-85937-203-1	£9.99
Nottinghamshire (pb)	1-85937-187-6	£9.99	Welsh Castles (pb)	1-85937-322-4	£9.99
Oxford (pb)	1-85937-411-5	£9.99	West Midlands (pb)	1-85937-289-9	£9.99
Oxfordshire (pb)	1-85937-430-1	£9.99	West Sussex	1-85937-148-5	£14.99
Peak District (pb)	1-85937-280-5	£9.99	West Yorkshire (pb)	1-85937-201-5	£9.99
Penzance	1-85937-069-1	£12.99	Weymouth (pb)	1-85937-209-0	£9.99
Peterborough (pb)	1-85937-219-8	£9.99	Wiltshire (pb)	1-85937-277-5	£9.99
Piers	1-85937-237-6	£17.99	Wiltshire Churches (pb)	1-85937-171-x	£9.99
Plymouth	1-85937-119-1	£12.99	Wiltshire Living Memories	1-85937-245-7	£14.99
Poole & Sandbanks (pb)	1-85937-251-1	£9.99	Winchester (pb)	1-85937-428-x	£9.99
Preston (pb)	1-85937-212-0	£9.99	Windmills & Watermills	1-85937-242-2	£17.99
Reading (pb)	1-85937-238-4	£9.99	Worcester (pb)	1-85937-165-5	£9.99
Romford (pb)	1-85937-319-4	£9.99	Worcestershire	1-85937-152-3	£14.99
Salisbury (pb)	1-85937-239-2	£9.99	York (pb)	1-85937-199-x	£9.99
Scarborough (pb)	1-85937-379-8	£9.99	Yorkshire (pb)	1-85937-186-8	£9.99
St Albans (pb)	1-85937-341-0	£9.99	Yorkshire Living Memories	1-85937-166-3	£14.99

See Frith books on the internet www.francisfrith.co.uk

FRITH PRODUCTS & SERVICES

Francis Frith would doubtless be pleased to know that the pioneering publishing venture he started in 1860 still continues today. A hundred and forty years later, The Francis Frith Collection continues in the same innovative tradition and is now one of the foremost publishers of vintage photographs in the world. Some of the current activities include:

Interior Decoration

Today Frith's photographs can be seen framed and as giant wall murals in thousands of pubs, restaurants, hotels, banks, retail stores and other public buildings throughout the country. In every case they enhance the unique local atmosphere of the places they depict and provide reminders of gentler days in an increasingly busy and frenetic world.

Product Promotions

Frith products are used by many major companies to promote the sales of their own products or to reinforce their own history and heritage. Frith promotions have been used by Hovis bread, Courage beers, Scots Porage Oats, Colman's mustard, Cadbury's foods, Mellow Birds coffee, Dunhill pipe tobacco, Guinness, and Bulmer's Cider.

Genealogy and Family History

As the interest in family history and roots grows world-wide, more and more people are turning to Frith's photographs of Great Britain for images of the towns, villages and streets where their ancestors lived; and, of course, photographs of the churches and chapels where their ancestors were christened, married and buried are an essential part of every genealogy tree and family album.

Frith Products

All Frith photographs are available Framed or just as Mounted Prints and Posters (size 23 x 16 inches). These may be ordered from the address below. From time to time other products - Address Books, Calendars, Table Mats, etc - are available.

The Internet

Already twenty thousand Frith photographs can be viewed and purchased on the internet through the Frith websites and a myriad of partner sites.

For more detailed information on Frith companies and products, look at these sites:

www.francisfrith.co.uk
www.francisfrith.com
(for North American visitors)

See the complete list of Frith Books at:

www.francisfrith.co.uk

This web site is regularly updated with the latest list of publications from the Frith Book Company. If you wish to buy books relating to another part of the country that your local bookshop does not stock, you may purchase on-line.

For further information, trade, or author enquiries please contact us at the address below:
The Francis Frith Collection, Frith's Barn, Teffont, Salisbury, Wiltshire, England SP3 5QP.
Tel: +44 (0)1722 716 376 Fax: +44 (0)1722 716 881 Email: sales@francisfrith.co.uk

See Frith books on the internet www.francisfrith.co.uk

TO RECEIVE YOUR FREE MOUNTED PRINT

Mounted Print
Overall size 14 x 11 inches

Cut out this Voucher and return it with your remittance for £1.95 to cover postage and handling, to UK addresses. For overseas addresses please include £4.00 post and handling. Choose any photograph included in this book. Your SEPIA print will be A4 in size, and mounted in a cream mount with burgundy rule line, overall size 14 x 11 inches.

Order additional Mounted Prints at HALF PRICE (only £7.49 each*)

If there are further pictures you would like to order, possibly as gifts for friends and family, purchase them at half price (no additional postage and handling required).

Have your Mounted Prints framed*

For an additional £14.95 per print you can have your chosen Mounted Print framed in an elegant polished wood and gilt moulding, overall size 16 x 13 inches (no additional postage and handling required).

---

* IMPORTANT!
These special prices are only available if ordered using the original voucher on this page (no copies permitted) and at the same time as your free Mounted Print, for delivery to the same address

---

Frith Collectors' Guild

From time to time we publish a magazine of news and stories about Frith photographs and further special offers of Frith products. If you would like 12 months FREE membership, please return this form.

Send completed forms to:
The Francis Frith Collection, Frith's Barn, Teffont, Salisbury, Wiltshire SP3 5QP

Voucher for FREE and Reduced Price Frith Prints

Picture no.	Page number	Qty	Mounted @ £7.49	Framed + £14.95	Total Cost
		1	**Free of charge***	£	£
			£7.49	£	£
			£7.49	£	£
			£7.49	£	£
			£7.49	£	£
			£7.49	£	£

Please allow 28 days for delivery	*** Post & handling**	**£1.95**
Book Title	**Total Order Cost**	**£**

Please do not photocopy this voucher. Only the original is valid, so please cut it out and return it to us.

I enclose a cheque / postal order for £ . . . .
made payable to 'The Francis Frith Collection'
OR please debit my Mastercard / Visa / Switch / Amex card
(credit cards please on all overseas orders)

Number . . . .

Issue No(Switch only) . . . . .Valid from (Amex/Switch) . . . .

Expires . . . . Signature . . . .

Name Mr/Mrs/Ms . . . .

Address . . . .

. . . .

. . . . Postcode . . . .

Daytime Tel No . . . .   Valid to 31/12/02

The Francis Frith Collectors' Guild

Please enrol me as a member for 12 months free of charge.

Name Mr/Mrs/Ms . . . .

Address . . . .

. . . .

. . . . Postcode . . . .

Would you like to find out more about Francis Frith?

We have recently recruited some entertaining speakers who are happy to visit local groups, clubs and societies to give an illustrated talk documenting Frith's travels and photographs. If you are a member of such a group and are interested in hosting a presentation, we would love to hear from you.

Our speakers bring with them a small selection of our local town and county books, together with sample prints. They are happy to take orders. A small proportion of the order value is donated to the group who have hosted the presentation. The talks are therefore an excellent way of fundraising for small groups and societies.

Can you help us with information about any of the Frith photographs in this book?

We are gradually compiling an historical record for each of the photographs in the Frith archive. It is always fascinating to find out the names of the people shown in the pictures, as well as insights into the shops, buildings and other features depicted.

If you recognize anyone in the photographs in this book, or if you have information not already included in the author's caption, do let us know. We would love to hear from you, and will try to publish it in future books or articles.

Our production team

Frith books are produced by a small dedicated team at offices in the converted Grade II listed 18th-century barn at Teffont near Salisbury, illustrated above. Most have worked with the Frith Collection for many years. All have in common one quality: they have a passion for the Frith Collection. The team is constantly expanding, but currently includes:

Jason Buck, John Buck, Douglas Burns, Heather Crisp, Isobel Hall, Rob Hames, Hazel Heaton, Peter Horne, James Kinnear, Tina Leary, Hannah Marsh, Eliza Sackett, Terence Sackett, Sandra Sanger, Shelley Tolcher, Susanna Walker, Clive Wathen and Jenny Wathen.

Free Print - see overleaf